THE GAME CHANGER

Thanks to the Creative Team:

Kerri Morrison

Hamish MacDonald

Shannon Waller

Jennifer Bhatthal

Christine Nishino

Willard Bond

Paul Hamilton

Cartoons by Hamish MacDonald.

Printed in Toronto, Canada. The Strategic Coach Inc., 33 Fraser Avenue, Suite 201, Toronto, Ontario, M6K 3J9.

This publication is meant to strengthen your common sense, not to substitute for it. It is also not a substitute for the advice of your doctor, lawyer, accountant, or any of your advisors, personal or professional.

If you would like further information about the Strategic Coach® Program or other Strategic Coach® services and products, please telephone 416.531.7399 or 1.800.387.3206.

Library and Archives Canada Cataloguing in Publication

Sullivan, Dan, 1944-, author
        The game changer / Dan Sullivan.

ISBN 978-1-897239-44-5 (paperback)

1. Leadership. 2. Entrepreneurship. I. Title.

HD57.7.S777 2016   658.4'092   C2015-908551-9

Contents

Introduction
Adopting Eight Game-Changer Mindsets

The word "game" is typically used in the context of sports or entertainment. But for the past few decades, it has become more commonly used in business: *"The game" is whatever marketplace or industry you're in, or a particular type of product or service. It's how well you manage your business to be productive, profitable, and competitive.*

Tremendous jump in value creation.

As in sports or entertainment, you're competing with other players in your game. The same rule—that there are winners and losers—comes into the business realm. The analogy of business as a game is so common now that if you say something is a "game changer," most people no longer think in terms of sports; rather, they know it to mean that somebody did *something entirely new and innovative to provide a tremendous jump in value creation within a marketplace that disproportionately rewards the person who made the change.*

Because this person is being rewarded with attention and market share, they cause so much unbalance in a particular marketplace or industry that everybody else must adapt to the changes—or lose out. More and more, in the business world, the leaders are those who can disrupt an existing game with something new that changes the rules of competition in their marketplace.

Whole industries suddenly and rapidly disrupted.

There are many examples of this disruption: The movement from analog to digital shook things up in the recording industry, which had been based on analog technology. All of a sudden, digital came into the picture, and it was much cheaper, the equipment was easier to produce, it was easier to use, and it was available to a much wider market.

In only a few years, the entire analog recording industry was gone. Now, it's coming back, but as a novelty or luxury item. Things don't necessarily disappear forever but can return as a niche type of product. The main market, however, has now been taken over by a new change in the game.

Another example is the microelectronic revolution, with the microchip being applied to products and services that didn't previously make use of it. One of the most recent examples is Uber, which introduced a smartphone app that essentially eliminated all the middle people and middle methods that had been part of the transportation industry by directly linking a customer with a driver with no money spent on either of them searching for each other.

All the time wasted in customers looking for a ride and drivers looking for a passenger was eliminated. It's such a disproportionate advantage that it's radically transforming what is an old, accepted industry, going back to horse and buggy days. There have always been taxis and drivers. Now, this new technology has completely disrupted the industry in a matter of about five years.

Entirely new organizing ideas and methods.
Game changers aren't always technological. Sometimes, they're ideas, though they usually have a teamwork and technology component. An example is an idea like "Just In Time" manufacturing, which means keeping low inventory and receiving parts or goods for your business only as you need them. Technology and teamwork developed as part of this process, but we wouldn't have had the technology if the

idea weren't there first.

The Japanese developed this strategy after the Second World War. It came about because of the density of population in Japan and the close proximity of the factories. After winning the war, the United States had vast productive capabilities that the Japanese didn't. The Japanese looked for any way to gain an advantage and increase speed of production. They decided to have parts arrive only when they were needed, eliminating inventory and other costs.

Even without using modern means of conveyance or technology, they could deliver products the same day they were ordered. They could be produced and delivered in a matter of hours, so they didn't have to run big inventories. This was done in a manual fashion before it ever became technology-driven. They knew they had to find some way of competing. They were losing the game, and they wanted to get back into it. They introduced an entirely new way of organizing manufacturing processes and supplying products. And it started with a game-changing idea.

Replacing complexity with simplicity.
Generally, entrepreneurism starts with an idea. If you look at Strategic Coach, our Program is based on the idea that the essential problem for entrepreneurs is that they are very smart and creative people who have way too much going on in their heads. Therefore, if you can introduce them to new ways of thinking in relationship to different kinds of situations, freeing them up from complexity and confusion, they will use their natural intelligence and creativity to produce breakthrough results.

I realized it's not about giving them something *more*. It's actually about taking a lot away. To this day, most coaching programs will load people up with knowledge and "stuff." We say, entrepreneurs already have too much to think about, so we're going to go in the opposite direction. Oftentimes, a disruptive, game-changing idea takes advantage of a complex situation and makes things very, very simple.

At Strategic Coach, we take obstacles and turn them into an advantage. That's a game changer. Everybody's looking in one direction, and I look in the other. Indeed, Strategic Coach, from start to finish, has always consisted of a series of *thinking* game changers that take what everybody's looking at and present a totally different way of approaching it. It's the new way of looking at it that suddenly creates advantages and breakthroughs. Nothing is needed except a shift in people's perspective. For us, that's what the game changer is.

Mindsets that change the game for everyone.

Talking about marketplace activities as a game in this way puts a premium on coming up with disruptive ideas that change the game for everybody. Once the change is made, the entrepreneurial winners of the game are those who can adapt most quickly.

If you want to be a game changer, you have to think in new, unique, and much simpler ways. Changing your game, therefore, involves changing your mindset.

In the following eight chapters, I'll discuss the new and unique mindsets to adopt to become a game changer in your industry.

Chapter 1
No More Competition
Your biggest competitors find your creativity so valuable, they become your best customers.

The game changes suddenly when you stop competing.

One of the most crucial mindsets for a game changer to adopt is to simply stop thinking in terms of competition. Not only is it necessary to stop thinking about it, it's important to change the value creation proposition of your business to be to create so much value for your biggest and most powerful competitors that they actually become your biggest customers and promoters.

In many entrepreneurial programs in universities and colleges, students are taught that business is all about competition and, therefore, they will have to compete in the market based on price. They're told there's no other way to succeed in business.

But what happens with this obsession with competition is that it continually drives creativity and profitability out of the marketplace.

Everyone is anxiously fighting over scarcity.
Right now, very few of your competitors are feeling good about operating in a highly competitive market. They don't like the life they have to lead. They don't like the way they have to run their business. They don't like how they have to treat their customers. They don't like how they have to treat their staff. They're dealing with uncertain and anxious intensity all the time.

The reason this competition exists is that many people

believe there is only one pie for all of us and that it's a very small pie. There are too few pieces, and no one is going to be able to have a big enough piece upon which to build a satisfying life as an entrepreneur.

They think there's a scarcity of possibilities out there, and it makes them hold their existing ideas very close to the vest. They get caught up in a zero-sum game, believing that if someone else wins, they lose.

This scarce and secretive mindset keeps them needlessly preoccupied with gaining short-range advantage in the marketplace and encourages envy, resentment, and jealousy, which undermine personal success.

Creating new ideas that make the pie bigger.

Looking at this situation, I decided that if everybody thinks it's a dog-eat-dog competition, I would create a way of feeding all the dogs.

I asked myself, "Why don't we simply make the pie a lot bigger?" And so I introduced a change in the game that would enlarge the pie. And not only that, but within any pie, there would be many different pies, adding dimensionality to the marketplace.

To do this, I made my business about ideas rather than about commodity sales that inevitably lead to competition based on price.

The marketplace for ideas is unlimited because there is no limitation on new ideas.

It's a lot easier to come up with new ideas than it is to come up with new products and services. And all products, services, and methods that are sold in the marketplace are the result of a particular set of ideas.

Rather than keeping my ideas secret, I realized that I don't lose anything by sharing my knowledge. In fact, I've likely enhanced my understanding of the ideas by sharing them with someone.

What we're seeing in the marketplace more and more—and this happens in local markets, in large markets, and on a global basis—is that *the level of cooperation among competitors is actually much higher than the amount of head-to-head competition.*

Solving the worst problems of competitors.

The first thing I do when I come up with an idea is to turn out a book, podcasts, and videos that take my idea and let it go out into the world. In my role as a creator within Strategic Coach, I'm always trying to produce ideas that are going to make it a lot easier for people who are competing with me to run better businesses as a result.

By starting with that mindset, I can't focus on the competition between myself and someone else. I look at how the whole industry can get better, and I become the expert on improving the industry that hundreds and thousands of people are involved in.

One of the most beautiful ways to be innovative is to think from the standpoint of the worst problems your competitor has and solve them.

In this way, you give up all the fear associated with the notion that your competitors are going to steal your ideas. Instead, you become known. You become the person who educates your whole industry. In any marketplace, there is no better position to be in.

Playing the game in a completely different way.

My goal is to be an educator whose lessons can benefit anyone. I would love it if all my competitors benefited from my new ideas, new approaches, new strategies, and new ways of thinking.

Having this mindset and approach to business changes the game for me. I'm playing the game in a completely different way than anyone else because no one else is trying to share and solve the problems of their competitors.

By helping your competitors, they'll get better—and that's good for the marketplace. The reputation of the industry goes up. You're creating a richer environment.

I decided a long time ago that I didn't want to play the anxiety game. I didn't want to play the scarcity game. I don't want to think about my competition except to solve their problems.

I want to focus only on creating value—first of all, for our own clients and customers, and then for those who think they're in competition with me.

The best way to play the game is to not worry about your competition. Just go ahead and innovate, and you'll turn would-be competitors into loyal customers.

Chapter 2
Test Only On Check Writers
You waste no time, testing your new ideas directly in the marketplace and getting useful feedback from the right audience.

Many entrepreneurs, when they come up with a new idea, will test it on their employees, their spouse, their children, their college buddy, their lawyer—but not on the people who would actually write them a check for their idea.

This comes from a fear of the reality of the marketplace and of the people who are in a position to write them a check. They'll go through elaborate preparations before they're "ready" to test their ideas in the marketplace. But it's a delaying process to postpone as long as possible the moment when they're actually going to have to present their idea to someone who is going to either accept or reject them by either writing a check or not writing a check.

Receiving a check is the only way to validate a new idea. Indeed, the only difference between a good idea and a bad idea is a check.

Never fall in love with your new ideas.
The truth is that most people with creative new ideas are scared silly of the marketplace because they fall in love with their own idea. One thing I've learned, though, is that until there is a check, there is no love. Until I receive a check, I'm merely "on a date" with the idea—I'm not married to it.

This fear of the marketplace is a fear of being rejected. It's a great act of courage to be willing to test your idea against someone who doesn't know you, someone who is purely self-interested, someone who either will or will not pay you for your idea. But if you don't test your ideas on check writers, there's no reality check.

It's vital not to develop strong emotions regarding your creation until you can confirm the validity of your idea and that somebody else is willing to write you a check for it. Never fall in love with your idea until check writers fall in love with it first.

No delay in testing against marketplace reality.
The concept of testing only on check writers has come from my 40 years of personal experience and observation of what happens when entrepreneurs test their new ideas on anyone other than the people who are actually going to write a check for them.

If you have what you believe is a winning, selling idea, go immediately to the person who would give you a win by giving you money for the idea. Any delay in doing this weakens the idea. If you try to test it on people who are not your ultimate audience, any feedback they give you is going to mislead you, undermine you, or discourage you.

In the entrepreneurial world, I often see business owners test their ideas on the people who work for them. But it's important to understand that, in most cases, the people who work for you are nervous about new ideas that won't immediately bring in cash flow, that won't guarantee their salary. This may be conscious or unconscious on their part, but they are likely to have a lower risk tolerance for new ideas than you have. Not only that, but when you test a Front Stage idea intended for clients on a Back Stage audience like your team members, they're less likely to "get it."

When you don't test ideas on the right audience, you're going to get a lot of confusing feedback, and it's not going to be valuable. It's not going to be information that improves the quality of your product. After they have given their feedback, you are no closer to knowing whether you have a winning idea than you were before you brought it to them.

Let potential check writers transform your idea.

This is also the case when you bring your ideas to people in your personal life. Your spouse, your brother-in-law, the people you drink with at the bar—these are not good people to test new ideas on.

There is only one individual to test an idea on, and that's someone who is in the immediate position, if they really like it, to say, "I'd pay you $10,000 for that." Or, even better, "I'd pay you $10,000 if you just change this, and this, and this." Any feedback you get from a check writer is incredibly valuable because it improves the idea—they are telling you how to make it practical and easy for them. It means you have a great idea, but not in the form you're planning to deliver it. *The marketplace will tell you exactly how they want it delivered.*

They want the value from your idea—they want something faster, easier, cheaper, and bigger—but they don't want you to make them work to get it. They're going to say, "If you solve this problem and make it easier to use, I'll write you a check for it."

The marketplace becomes your R&D partner.

Ultimately, your clients and customers—your only real audience—are the people to incorporate in your research and development, as they will give you useful feedback about whether your idea has value in the marketplace. Any R&D you do that's not with a check writer can be injurious to your future by wasting your time and supplying you with bad advice.

Always start by testing your ideas on those whose rejection will immediately set you into the mode of improvement. Once you have a few noes from the right audience, you can determine that you're going down the wrong road or have misjudged the market. But whether the response is positive or negative, if it's from the right audience—potential check writers—then it's real. They are the only people who have a vote. There are no other voters except for the marketplace, because only the marketplace has reality to it.

Yes and no are valuable, but maybe kills you.

I see people who angst over their ideas and delay for years actually taking their idea to the marketplace. The danger here for them is that while they're waiting, the marketplace changes. The marketplace for whom their idea was intended doesn't exist anymore.

This fear of rejection does you no favors. The sooner you get feedback from the right audience, the sooner you can move forward. Yeses reward you and noes teach you, but maybes kill you. And if you delay testing your idea in the marketplace, you're in a perpetual state of maybe.

The vast majority of entrepreneurs never realize the crucial importance of this approach to situations. This is why many of them achieve only modest or mediocre success over the course of their careers. Game changers are those who sur-pass mediocrity by eliminating all possibility of maybe.

Chapter 3
The Optimum Maximizer
You determine the optimum mindsets of those individuals who most maximize the best value you create in the world—and focus only on them.

If game changers are not going to indulge in competition, as I talked about in chapter 1, there needs to be a replacement for creating opportunity and cash.

The purpose of competition within industries is, to a certain extent, for entrepreneurs to create opportunities and cash out of people who are not like-minded. The only way to do that is by commoditizing your value creation. In other words, you have to bring your value creation down to a bare minimum where it would appeal to those who aren't like-minded, but only for one reason—that it's cheaper.

But if we don't have to compete, and we don't have to commoditize, then we're free to go to the other end of this spectrum. This is where we're going to make an entire marketplace out of people who are like-minded—people who have mindsets that are totally geared to what we're creating and are, therefore, in a position to take advantage to the maximum degree of what we're offering in the marketplace.

Creating your growing like-minded market.
We have to clearly establish the type of individual in the marketplace who's always going to be perfect for us—not just perfect now, but perfect forever.

Mindset is at the core of the issue. If you can determine the optimum mindsets of your best customers and market your offering directly to them, then everything else is easy.

In order to identify these mindsets, start by listing your three best experiences and three worst experiences with clients or prospects. Then determine the top eight mindsets that your best clients have in common. These mindsets become the criteria that tell you if someone is the right individual to be marketing your game-changing ideas to—in other words, if they are your *Optimum Maximizer*.

Optimum Maximizers are those customers and clients who possess the *optimum* mindsets to most *maximize* your value creation in the marketplace.

The way to determine which of your prospects possess these optimum mindsets is to create a mindset scorecard that lays out a spectrum of mindsets and acts as a framework for them to self-identify as a right-fit client for you.

Determining right-fit clientele by these mindsets distinguishes game-changing entrepreneurs from conventionally successful entrepreneurs. This is the marketing system for game changers.

Here are the eight optimum mindset characteristics of game changer clients who want to work with me: 1. Big Ambition, 2. Always Growing, 3. Courageous Risk-Taker, 4. Willing To Change, 5. Team Player, 6. Total Perseverance, 7. Creative Tester, and 8. Creative Reciprocity. I know that someone who meets these criteria is a like-minded individual who can best take advantage of the value I offer in the marketplace.

Who you are looking for is actually *you*.
Once you have created your scorecard and drafted your eight mindsets, what you begin to realize is that the clients

you most enjoy working with, the ones you most want to find in the marketplace, are the ones whose top eight mindsets most resemble and duplicate your own.

These are the individuals who will always make maximum use of your very best value creation on an ongoing basis. No matter what new things you innovate, they are always the ones who are most eager to make it their own and use it to develop and expand their own entrepreneurial success.

You can now focus entirely on creating for and marketing to check writers who are like-minded in the most fundamental ways. You no longer have to twist who you are into an artificial shape in order to attract check writers you only end up not liking. You no longer have to try to make yourself look good to people who don't look good to you.

Maximizers are always self-transforming.

Your eight mindsets define entrepreneurs and check writers who are "transformative." This means maximizing individuals who have the following transformative qualities:

• **Self-organizing:** Throughout their lives, they have been developing an internal organizing structure that is relatively oblivious to external roles, rules, requirements, restrictions, and rewards.

• **Self-generating:** These transformative individuals are also motivated by internal purposes that are uniquely inspiring and meaningful to them. They experience all growth and progress with a personally generated sense of recognition, approval, and satisfaction.

• **Self-evolving and self-inventing:** Finally, they are also uniquely transformative in that they continually maximize the value of their past experiences in order to multiply the value of their future capabilities, resources, and opportunities. They also always find greater value in their own lessons than in lessons they receive from others.

"Optimum statements" that differentiate you.

The mindset statements that are rated highest in your scorecard are what I call "optimum statements." You've made certain statements that define the mindsets of your best clients, and if the statements ring true for your prospects and accurately describe who they are, they will be attracted to you and will want to know more.

This marketing approach takes away all the hit-or-miss guesswork of finding and attracting the right clients. So many entrepreneurs try to gear their message to attract everybody, but you don't want everybody. You want to attract the *right people*. You want to know whom to talk to and whom not to talk to.

Creating your mindset scorecard.

Using the Optimum Maximizer concept, you're doing an enormous amount of disqualification right off the bat. I believe the key skill in sales is not qualifying—it's disqualifying. *The Optimum Maximizer criteria act as a filter that brings you only the best, right-fit clients.* Developing your own mindset scorecard using your Optimum Maximizer criteria is a crucial tool in becoming a game changer.

For an example of what these mindset scorecards look like, refer to the complete pullout of the back cover of this book, which provides the foundation for The 10x Ambition Program in Strategic Coach.

Chapter 4
Stockpile Multipliers
You know that changing the game requires six powerful, expanding marketplace forces.

Most entrepreneurs think cash is their biggest multiplier, but game changers know that five other multipliers are necessary to increase the power of cash.

In the previous three chapters, I described how game changers think differently from other entrepreneurs. We can now plot out how they multiply the power and impact of their game-changing ideas in the world.

Changing your game in any marketplace will always require six entrepreneurial multipliers: capabilities, creativity, credibility, connections, confidence, and cash. By "multiplier," I mean *a marketplace force that continually expands entrepreneurial advantage.*

Cash is an obvious multiplier advantage for all entrepreneurs, but for game changers, cash is actually the last one of the six to focus on. The more you focus on the first five "C's," the greater the amount of cash that will always be available to you.

Low cost and invisible. The two biggest reasons why the first five multipliers come first is that, one, in the 21st century, they don't require a lot of cash to obtain, and two, you can develop them *invisibly.*

The first 5 C's grow deceptively.
The first five multipliers—capabilities, creativity, credibility, connections, and confidence—all grow as a powerful integrated system in ways that are invisible to anyone outside

of a game changer's company and even to people inside of the company, aside from the entrepreneur. This is another way in which game-changing entrepreneurs can stop competing in the marketplace: No one else knows what they're doing—they're essentially operating in a secret dimension of progress and growth.

This means that, as a game changer, rather than competing, you only have to focus on developing and expanding six multiplier forces for the rest of your entrepreneurial life.

How 21st-century capabilities expand.
We're living in an increasingly technological world. As such, for entrepreneurial game changers, their most powerful capabilities will increasingly take the form of "technology teamwork."

In other words, it's not just technology, and it's not just teamwork, but the two continually combine in such a way that the Unique Ability of each individual is multiplied by that of everyone else, and all of these combined abilities are multiplied further by taking advantage of cutting-edge technological tools, systems, and networks around the world.

Capabilities x Creativity = Credibility
Anytime you have Unique Ability Teamwork being multiplied by accelerating technology, the automatic result is new creativity in the form of more productive concepts, methods, processes, tools, products, and services in a specific marketplace. If this describes your entrepreneurial company, then invariably your combination of capabilities and creativity will make you a game changer in your marketplace and industry.

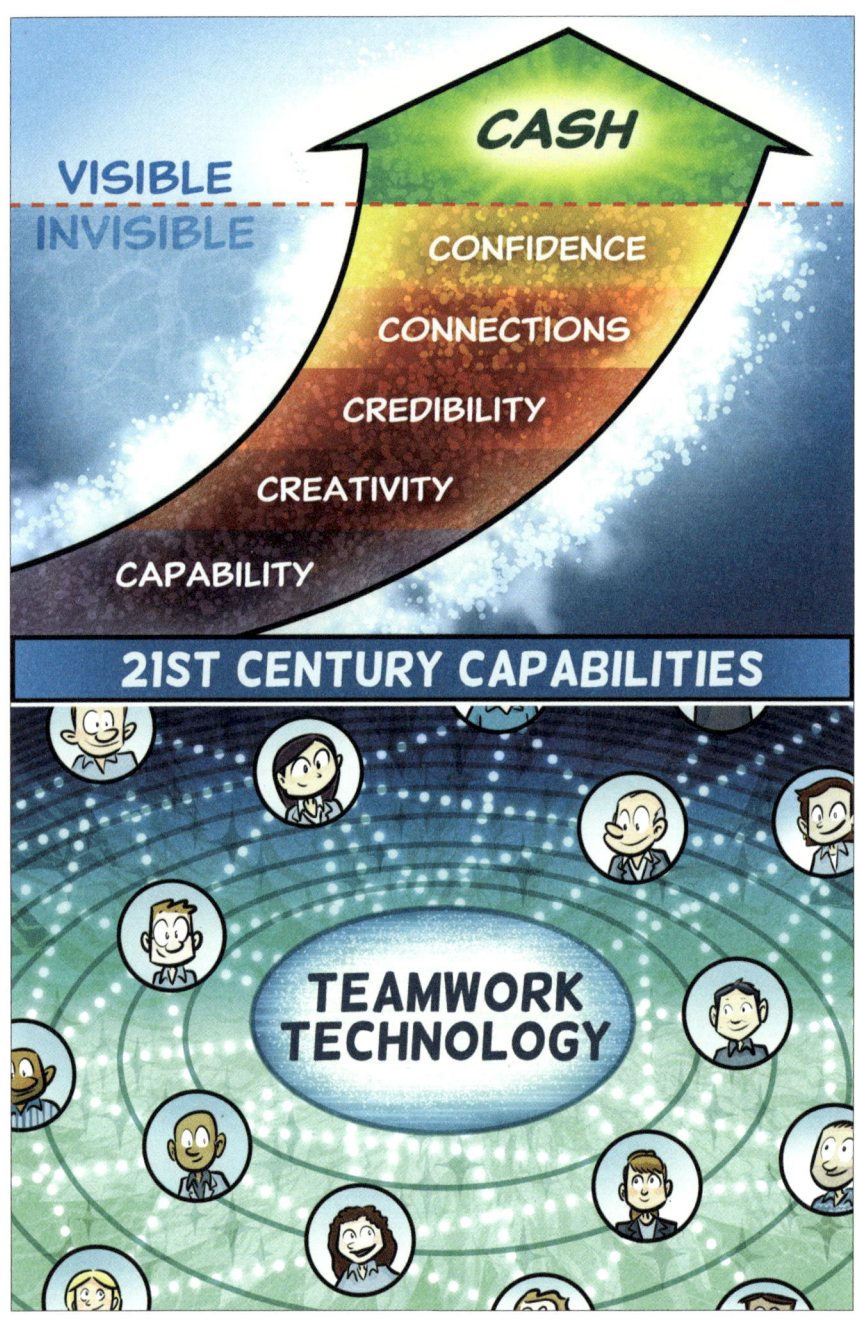

And because your technology-teamwork capability is always growing, your company's creativity also grows along with your reputation for innovative solutions that transform the way everybody views you from the outside.

Your credibility as a game changer expands in a uniquely permanent way because you understand where everything starts in this multiplier process— with technology-teamwork, which always generates greater creativity that produces an increasing flow of game-changing innovations.

Connections x Confidence = Cash

Your expanding credibility as a game changer in today's world leads to global connections with those who are attracted to your unique value creation solutions. This is the extraordinary payoff of living in an electronically-networked world in the 21st century:

As you increasingly prove that you're a game changer, everyone who is important for you to know will want to learn more about you and your innovations.

With expanding connections comes an increasing marketplace confidence in yourself and your company. Larger numbers of clients and prospects have a growing confidence in your ability to create value for them in areas that are crucial for their own progress, growth, and success.

The growing connections and confidence are mutually reinforcing: The greater the number of connections, the greater people's overall confidence in you becomes; and the more the confidence grows, the more the connections expand.

We are now arriving back above the "visibility line" at cash. Beneath the line, you can now see your first five multipliers as a connected series of ever-expanding game changer forces that produce increasing revenues and profits.

Everybody understands the cash result, but only game-changing entrepreneurs understand the five multiplier forces that permanently produce it.

Using cash to multiply the other 5 C's.

The cash multiplier now loops back down below the line to the beginning of the multiplier circuit, like a snake eating its tail—except that your increasing cash reinforces all of the first five multipliers simultaneously. What you see here is a closed-loop growth system that continually self-develops and self-expands into greater marketplace importance.

Here is what we have been putting together so far in this Game Changer book: In chapter 1, we talked about you as a game changer switching from a focus on competition to a focus on solving the problems of your biggest marketplace competitors. Next, in chapter 2, we talked about testing your innovative ideas and solutions only on check writers. And then in chapter 3, we talked about the best check writers being the "Optimum Maximizer" clients and customers.

Each of these is a game-changing mindset whose importance will now be magnified in your 6 C's multiplier system. As you master the reciprocal relationships among these six multipliers, you can ignore everything except those things that help to develop and expand your 6 C's in relation to your Optimum Maximizer clients.

Chapter 5
Expand Your Freedom

Your game changer impact continually grows from expanding your Four Freedoms of time, money, relationship, and purpose.

The overriding reason people become entrepreneurs is to gain increasing personal freedom in all areas of their lives over the course of their entire lifetimes.

But most discussions of innovation and game-changing ideas focus almost entirely on internal business capabilities and external marketing impacts—with no mention that all of these capabilities and impacts are by-products of an entrepreneur's growth of personal freedom.

Time, money, relationship, and purpose.

I'm a better entrepreneur and a better person to the degree that I can expand my own personal freedom. There are four areas of freedom that are crucial for entrepreneurs to master in order to be game changers.

Freedom of Time: I get to spend all my time doing what I love doing, and the time I spend doing what I love is devoted to the most important thing for the growth of the company. I spend my time doing activities that are innovative, not repetitive; new, not old.

Freedom of Money: We're making money in a way that's enjoyable, and everybody in the organization feels good about the way it's made. There's a sense that the money we make is modest in relation to the value we create in the marketplace. The transformation we create for a lot of people in their entrepreneurial lives is massively larger than the amount of money we charge for it. The money always increases because the value we create constantly increases.

Freedom of Relationship: At this point in my life and career, I never spend time with anyone—in Strategic Coach, outside Strategic Coach, in the marketplace—whose company I don't enjoy. The depth of my relationships with people strengthens my business relationships with them, but it's not for that purpose. I choose these relationships because of the content of them—I just enjoy the person.

Freedom of Purpose: Our purpose is not swayed by anybody else's agenda or by any outside circumstances. Strategic Coach is in the business of expanding entrepreneurial freedom, and the best way to be a good expander of other people's freedom is to continually expand your own freedom.

Your 10x bypass of others' approval and control.

These Four Freedoms are vital to being a game changer—there can be no force outside of yourself that's controlling the growth and progress of your company. It must all be internally generated. The growth of your creativity and capabilities cannot depend on the approval of anyone outside your company. There can be no one out there whose approval of you matters in the least. To be a game changer, you can't be beholden to anyone.

Non-entrepreneurs, entrepreneurs, and game changers experience three different levels of freedom. Entrepreneurs have more freedom of time, money, relationship, and purpose than the majority of non-entrepreneurs—often 10x more. The same difference exists between "regular" entrepreneurs and game-changing entrepreneurs: Game changers have 10x more freedom.

Indeed, there is a transformative connection between entrepreneurs' increasing personal freedom and their emergence as game changers in their markets and industries.

Your company as a game-changing vehicle.
But don't think this increased freedom means a lack of commitment or investment. On the contrary, it means the freedom to invest fully. I don't try to minimize the investment I'm making in my business so I can do the "real" stuff of life; instead, I've built my company to be a vehicle for growing personal freedom. The purpose of the company isn't to generate cash so that I can buy freedom outside of it. I have freedom within my business to do what I love.

Because Freedom of Purpose is included in the philosophy behind my company, I'm able to do what I want to do with my life *within* the company. I get to make the impact I want to make in the world as part of the company. There's nothing else aside from Coach for me and what happens inside Coach. All my freedom is experienced now, not later.

"Retirement" becomes a silly thought.
Someone in the corporate, bureaucratic world who's working in a job to make money for their family—to buy freedom, to buy capability, to buy a house and their children's education—often doesn't have the freedom of doing what they love. Their job is just a means to an end. It's something they do in exchange for something else so they can be freed up.

Those in this state can become increasingly angry and bitter that their career and personal life are frustrating and unrewarding. They're always working harder and longer so they can retire as soon as possible from work they don't like so they can finally experience freedom.

But the desire to retire means that they will continue to do only what they already know how to do. They will only do things that will safely contribute to their ability to retire, and anything new would simply represent a delay toward that retirement. The last thing they want to do when they're working only to retire is to suddenly discover something exciting at work. Game-changing breakthroughs are not what they're looking for.

A game changer mentality, however, is what actually leads to freedom *right now*. Through your creativity and innovations, you find you have a meaningful purpose that makes work enjoyable in and of itself. You aren't working to be freed up later. And with the continual expansion of your Four Freedoms in every area of life, retirement—essentially, being taken out of use—becomes an absurd thought.

Game changers are freedom role models.

In the 21st century, game-changing entrepreneurs are increasingly the role models for individual human development over the course of a lifetime. They occupy this position because millions of other people perceive the game changers to have extraordinary personal freedom—of time, money, relationship, and purpose.

The more one becomes a game changer, the more one's individual freedom expands; and the more one consciously expands their individual freedom, the more one becomes a game changer.

Chapter 6
Innovation Manager Breakthrough

Your emerging game changer ideas continually multiply and become real because of your growing Innovation Manager Breakthrough.

Game changers are typically very good at coming up with new ideas, but not necessarily good at taking those new ideas and making them real or making them recur.

What a game changer wants is someone whose joy in life is to take the game changer's new, creative ideas and make them real in terms of teamwork, methods, and processes.

They want the ability to have their game-changing ideas gain traction in reality.

Problem-solvers who make your ideas real.

More often than not, the innovator is not the person who can do that. The innovator is good at making up the ideas, but it's best to allow someone else to manage the ideas and make them happen.

The greatest frustration I've seen on the part of creative entrepreneurs is the absence of what I call an "Innovation Manager" in their business.

Your Innovation Manager is a highly responsive team member who loves transforming your game-changing ideas into practical action. They are skilled at integrating all the organizational abilities and resources that are crucial to progress in the marketplace.

When you transfer your idea to an Innovation Manager, they take your vision and see everything that needs to happen to give it an impactful, practical life in the real world.

You *make it up*, but the Innovation Manager *makes it real*.

Staying on your side of the innovation line.
Innovation Managers can pull together teams of people and give them the complete game plan to accomplish the task. They know exactly how to set up the structures and bring the right talent on board to make your ideas a reality.

I'm really good at seeing and defining new possibilities, but I'm not as good at taking the new possibility and moving it into teamwork and into organized structures and processes that will not only make it real but, if it's a success, set it up to make it recur.

My Innovation Managers, Cathy Davis and Paul Hamilton, are brilliant at this. And a big breakthrough for me was recognizing this and making sure to stay on my side of the line and in my area of Unique Ability without crossing into theirs.

No Innovation Manager, no game changer.
If a game changer doesn't have an Innovation Manager, their ideas simply don't go anywhere. They might have a game-changing idea, but they'll be frustrated because they'll have no support system for implementing it.

Not having an Innovation Manager completely holds back growth and prevents your game-changing ideas from coming to life.

And an idea is only a game changer if it becomes real in the marketplace.

The most powerful idea in the world that's not made real is worthless. Many innovative entrepreneurs spend their careers in a cycle of frustration, futility, and failure because they never understand the crucial role of the Innovation Manager. The ideas keep coming but few if any of them have any practical impact outside of their imagination.

The majority of innovative entrepreneurs have no transformative impact on their markets and industries because they lack this crucial organizational capability.

Make it up, make it real, make it recur.

One mistake many entrepreneurs make is that they bring their ideas to the wrong person in their company. They get excited about a new idea they have, and they bring it to what I call a Process Manager instead of an Innovation Manager. But these are very different types of managers.

When you give a Process Manager a new idea, their inclination is to put it at the bottom of their list because they already have a list of established processes that they feel take priority over something new.

The inclination of an Innovation Manager, on the other hand, regardless of what they have on their list, is to put your idea at the top because it's new. Today's idea is a lot more exciting to them than a three-day-old idea. They like new ideas, but they don't want to repeat the new ideas.

That's where the Process Manager comes in. Their job is to take existing processes and improve the quality and the efficiency of them. Innovation Managers default to what's new; Process Managers default to what's existing.

Both of these types of managers are vital to your organization, but it's important to bring your projects, ideas, and tasks to the right one.

As an entrepreneur, you *make it up*, your Innovation Manager *makes it real*, and your Process Manager *makes it recur*.

The person you want to be most connected to in your organization is an Innovation Manager, not a Process Manager. When you bring your ideas to an Innovation Manager, you get support and enthusiasm. If you bring your ideas to a Process Manager first, you'll likely end up feeling discouraged and disappointed because a Process Manager is more skeptical of something new and has to first determine how the new idea will fit into their process before they can be excited about it.

In order to protect your confidence, bring your new ideas to an Innovation Manager who will be excited about them and want to put them into play.

Your Self-Multiplying Company future.

When you have an Innovation Manager—or a team of them—and an innovation system in place to make your ideas real, your overall company becomes self-multiplying. The Self-Multiplying Company is an exponentially more powerful idea for already 10x entrepreneurs who have game changer ambitions.

With an Innovation Manager, you have an organizational process that multiplies the value of each of your innovative ideas in the marketplace.

Chapter 7
Create New Multiplier Inequality
Your game changer solution creates massive inequality that forces everyone else to transform or leave the "game."

A game changer is the one who's first in with a brand new way of thinking and doing things that draws all the attention to them. Part of this attention involves making a lot more money.

Where the marketplace might have been in equilibrium before their new idea, the game changer suddenly creates incredible inequality.

There are many examples in the business world of somebody suddenly creating this massive inequality. BlackBerry controlled the mobile phone business when Apple came out with the iPhone. They pulled the rug out from under BlackBerry, shook up the industry, and did it in a way that nobody thought they could.

As the new game gets created, the creator of the disruption—the game changer—is going to massively succeed in a way that's not normal for the industry.

Multiplier inequality around the world.
You see this type of inequality around the world. There's a famous study of Nogales, Mexico, and Nogales, Arizona. They're across the Rio Grande river from each other. What the study found was that the individuals living in those two cities could have the same size family, be equally well educated, and be equally talented, but overall, the American who's only two miles away across the river is generally eight

times better off economically, as well as in terms of public safety, access to facilities, and so on, than the Mexican.

This is because the U.S. as an economic system creates massive inequality, which is also why many people complain about the United States and Canada—but everybody wants to come here.

When a country's emphasis is on innovation rather than equality, the overall result is greater individual opportunity to become more productive, profitable, and prosperous.

Game changers confidently multiply inequality.

Game changers create value that improves everything on the planet. But to be a true game changer, you have to be comfortable with the fact that what you're creating is going to result in massive inequality, at least in the short term, and know that in the long run, everyone will have an opportunity to benefit personally from your innovations.

Game changer entrepreneurs see everything and everyone in terms of individualism—their own and everyone else's—and are, consequently, immune to collectivist ideals, sensitivities, and obligations that prevent most people from being practically innovative.

The whole point of a game-changing innovation is to multiply inequalities of productivity and profitability in a particular situation. As a result of the new innovation, certain people suddenly get breakthrough advantages that make everyone else's capabilities obsolete and disrupt their confidence.

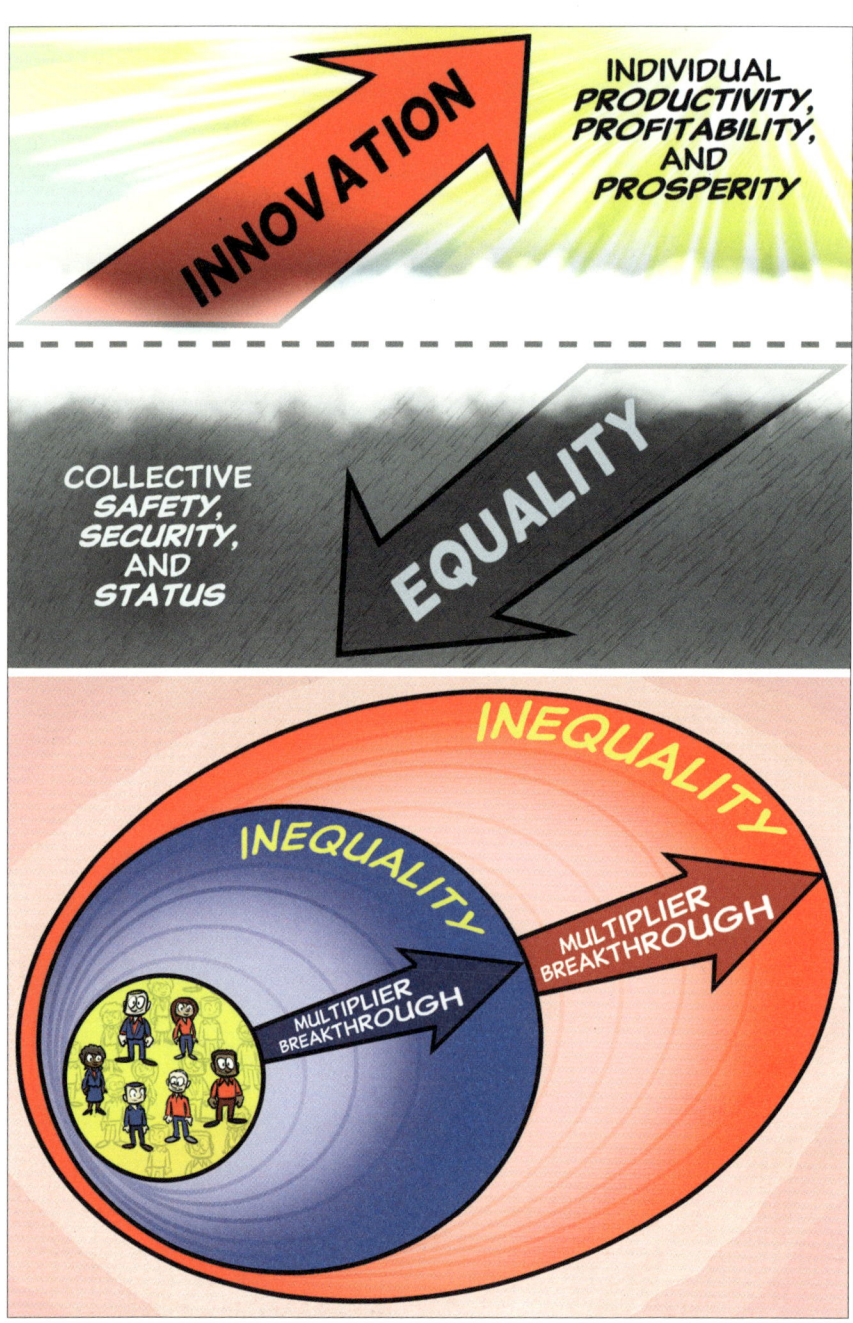

But all human progress is based on these sudden, massive inequalities. Progress is never made by protecting people.

Challenging people upward.

Progress is made by challenging people. A game changer idea challenges people to use their brains differently, to use their talents differently. It forces everybody else to transform —or leave the game.

Not everybody benefits from the inequality, but a lot more people benefit than don't. As an innovator, you can't think about the possible damage because the possible benefits are too great.

With major game changers, huge numbers of people are thrown out of work. Industries change. Whole towns disappear. Whole ways of life disappear. But the long-range benefit for everyone is exponentially greater.

America rewards multiplier breakthroughs.

A really big game change will create a lot of suffering and disruption, but the most advanced societies are the ones that least protect their people from that suffering. The U.S. is the number-one economy in the world because it's the country that least protects its citizens from personal failure.

It lets you go bankrupt. It doesn't protect you from losing your job or your home. It's unpredictable. It's harsh. But, ultimately, vastly more people benefit from it than are discomforted and disrupted by it.

All game changers have this disrupting impact. There is no change of game that doesn't hurt somebody. There is always somebody who is playing an old game that their income, reputation, pension, and power are tied to, and they are going to lose all that with the change of game.

You are not responsible for that. Things may be uncomfortable for a lot of people as a result of your game-changing innovation, but that discomfort doesn't signify that it shouldn't be done.

Ultimately, the majority will benefit from your innovations. And everything that is dynamic in American society encourages, supports, and rewards individual game changers who create these new multiplier breakthroughs.

Faster, easier, cheaper, and bigger results.
As a game changer, your focus is on innovative breakthroughs that will make things faster, easier, cheaper, and bigger for everyone on the planet.

Anyone who introduces new ways of doing things that combine these four characteristics will certainly create a disruptive breakthrough in an existing situation. And if this initial breakthrough keeps developing and expanding, it will automatically be a game changer.

Essentially, the opportunity to be a game changer of one kind or another is available to anyone who applies the faster-easier-cheaper-bigger formula to any area of practical activity, in any place on the planet, at any time.

The emergence of self-empowering digital tools, systems, and networks in the 21st century makes being a game changer in your immediate situation a growing possibility for an increasing number of entrepreneurial individuals.

Chapter 8
Game-Changing Community
Your ambition to be a game changer continually multiplies because of the increasing success of game changers around you.

To be a game changer, it's necessary to have a mindset that it's okay, for a while anyway, to be unpopular.

Game changers are innovators who introduce new ideas that disrupt the existing status quo of particular situations. They create something entirely new that's usually very "rude" when it makes its entrance, and is really quite careless about what it destroys when it gets there.

This means that their creativity invariably triggers non-acceptance and opposition on the part of those whose personal status is threatened by the game-changing innovation.

Create a like-minded market and community.
This is a normal response, and game changers can expect it as part of the innovation process. At the same time, the best way to neutralize the opposition is to create, from the earliest stages of the innovative process, a groundswell of enthusiastic support on the part of check-writing clients who are personally invested in the growing success of your game-changing breakthrough.

In effect then, one of the crucial skills of all aspiring game changers is to create their own unique marketplace at the same time as they are creating the unique breakthrough.

This unique marketplace consists of individuals whose mindsets most match those of the innovator, and their support not only includes funding to pay for the development and expansion of the game-changing idea, but enthusiastic promotion that counteracts and overcomes any and all opposition to the new breakthrough solution.

This new game changer marketplace is one dimension of the game-changing community that entrepreneurial game changers require. The other dimension that is equally important consists of other innovative entrepreneurs who are going through the same process of creating something that is new, better, and different. By definition, these other game changers will have a resonant set of mindsets that provide powerful encouragement, support, and inspiration.

The crucial importance of both dimensions of the game-changing community—paying clientele and fellow innovators—is that no entrepreneur can become a game changer as an isolated innovator. The image of the self-reliant, world-changing marketplace pioneer is unrealistic in the interconnected 21st century.

Game changing is entirely social.

Game changers are a unique breed. They may strive after breakthrough ideas rather than popularity, but they do need a community of like-minded people. There has to be a part of their life where they feel normal, where they're accepted.

Humans are social creatures. We're as much social creatures as fish are water creatures. Society is the water we swim in. Indeed, our lives are all about relationship, so it's vital to have people in our lives who think the way we do. For game changers, we need to be surrounded by people for whom having big goals and striving for exponential breakthroughs is normal.

WE CAN LEARN "SUCCESSFUL COURAGE" FROM OTHERS

4 CONFIDENCE

1 COMMITMENT

3 CAPABILITY

2 COURAGE

INNOVATION | CLIENTELE | COMMUNITY

CREATIVE RECIPROCITY

WILLING TO CHANGE

BIG AMBITION

TEAM PLAYER

ALWAYS GROWING

TOTAL PERSEVERANCE

RISK-TAKER

CREATIVE TESTER

BE THE BEST EXAMPLE OF
WHO YOU WANT TO ATTRACT

Without a community of fellow innovators, every day is hard work because the game changer's own mindsets are not being supported and encouraged in their marketplace activities. It's all they can do each day just to work up the energy and resolve to deal with people who are not like-minded.

Learning "successful courage" from others.

For some of our clients in The Strategic Coach Program, their quarterly workshops are the only days a year where they're in a space with like-minded people who don't see their big goals as being unusual or even too ambitious. Everyone in the room is just as excited about big changes and breakthrough goals as they are.

As entrepreneurs, our big vision ideas often put us in a position that requires courage to move forward. Being around other game changers makes these commitments and goals less scary and normalizes courage.

Every innovation that becomes a game changer starts with the *commitment* of individual people, followed by their willingness to go through a period of *courage*, which enables them to acquire new organizational and marketing *capabilities*, leading to increased entrepreneurial *confidence*.

Sharing this experience within a community of equally ambitious, like-minded people makes life more enjoyable.

A universe of game-changing R&D.

The most continually successful game-changing entrepreneurs in the 21st century will always be those with the most powerful game-changing communities.

We are all involved in a big R&D experiment, and different innovators have different methods of experimenting, which means their success can also be of benefit to us. The more people there are experimenting, the more possibilities there are to learn new methods without each of us having to do all the hard work ourselves to get the result.

A game-changing support community can be endlessly cultivated and expanded over an entire entrepreneurial career, with an accelerating payoff of innovative research and development in other marketplaces around the world.

Be the best example of who you want to attract.

Finding and attracting the right customers and clients, and building your game-changing community, starts with your marketing. You're looking for the mindsets that make prospects "like-minded." Your eight Optimum Maximizer mindsets define your market as well as your growth community.

What you say about your value creation proposition in the marketplace, and how you say it, reinforces and magnifies these mindsets. And, of course, if these are the mindsets you want to attract, then they have to be the mindsets you demonstrate in your own daily behavior.

Your best game changer innovations in the years ahead, those that will create the greatest marketplace value for the longest period of time, can be accelerated in their progress and multiplied in their impact to the degree that you become the best example of your Optimum Maximizer mindsets in everything you do.

Conclusion
A 25-Year Commitment
Your game changer platform is so superior that it creates an entirely new industry over the next 25 years.

Being a game changer requires a long-term commitment. It requires the instinct to want to change the world permanently in the direction of your game-changing idea.

This means being willing to put in 25 years to pull that off. It may not take you 25 years to achieve your goal, but having a 25-year commitment gives enough proof to others that this is something worth betting on.

If it's not important enough for you to commit 25 years to, it's not a game changer. If it doesn't stand the test of a 25-year commitment, you're not really serious about it.

Marketplace magic grows over 25 years.
Viewing your goals with a 25-year vision sharpens your focus on what has longevity. You focus on what can grow and what you're willing to invest in for that length of time.

Very few entrepreneurs in our fast-changing 21st-century business world can establish and maintain a 25-year commitment, but the most successful game changers always seem to have had a very long period of time before they became known for their success, when they maintained a single focus on pulling off something very important.

Although there are examples reported in the news media of new ideas and solutions that are described as having caused overnight breakthroughs in particular markets and industries, a closer examination usually reveals that, for a long time, the innovation was a development that few people could see. The media recognizes entrepreneurial game changers only when they start to generate cash. But before this occurs, five other rewards—capability, creativity, credibility, connections, and confidence—have to be developed, and each of these requires time. As an aspiring game changer, you have to be totally committed to taking whatever time is necessary to make the biggest possible and most profitable impact with your innovation.

I suggest 25 years as a very powerful and productive time commitment. If you give yourself this amount of time in which to produce a single game changer, you'll make sure that what you're creating is worth the commitment and that everything you're creating is thoroughly tested with check writers, each of whom will have provided you with feedback that supplies "market reality" to every stage of your game changer project.

Though it probably won't take 25 years for your game changer breakthrough to emerge, committing yourself for 25 years will guarantee that your breakthrough is a game changer.

Long enough for breakthroughs to be "normal."

For an innovation to be a game changer, it must be successful for a long enough period of time that everyone in the market considers it "normal." In fact, it must be considered so normal that most people can't remember how things were before the innovation changed the game.

In the world of popular culture and throughout the technological universe, the spotlight often shines on individuals

who create innovations that *seem* to be game changers. Frequently, there is a rush of publicity and money for these innovations, which richly reward the innovator, but the marketplace excitement doesn't last very long. The promise of something fundamentally bigger and better is not fulfilled. The innovator derives great value from the possibility of something new and different, but this doesn't translate into the reality of increased value for everyone else.

It's only if an innovative breakthrough continually creates greater value for an increasing number of individuals over a 25-year period that it can truly be considered a game changer.

Whole new approach = whole new industry.

Having a 25-year focus also puts you in a position to create an entirely new industry. You don't have to set out with this intention: It's a by-product of the magnitude of value you're creating.

All entrepreneurs want to be successful as individuals in their marketplace. Really successful entrepreneurs create companies that put them in the spotlight as leaders and role models for everyone else. But innovative entrepreneurs who introduce breakthrough solutions that transform the capabilities of all other entrepreneurs in their marketplace—and do this increasingly over 25 years—are the ones who create entirely new industries.

Microtechnology generates new games.

The term "game changer" is of fairly recent vintage, related first to sports in the 1980s, and then to the business, political, technological, and scientific worlds in the 1990s. A possible reason why it's a new term in daily discourse is that it was needed to describe the kinds of sudden changes that have accompanied the application of microtechnology in all areas of life, in all parts of the world.

Millions of people have a sense that the rules for living their lives, doing their work, and relating to each other are transforming in significant ways. Their "games" are changing. This growing perception, in turn, has brought to hero and celebrity status those innovative entrepreneurs who can create game changer solutions. These game changers in a growing number of arenas are increasingly valued as the most important and influential individuals in the world.

Game changing for 25 years is the goal.

There is entrepreneurism—and then there is game-changing entrepreneurism. The first is a powerful force in all markets. The second is a transformative movement on the planet. Anyone who chooses can embark on an entrepreneurial path tomorrow, but for any entrepreneur to become a game changer requires a 25-year commitment.

Moreover, you can't be a game changer because you're trying to get somewhere. Game changers are happy with the *activity*. This means being present in your daily life, right now. Whether your ideas become significant or not, whether you become famous for them or not, the activity of being a game changer is in itself the goal. It's what you want to do for the rest of your life.

As a game changer, there's no specific end point that I want to get to. I just want the next step to be more exciting than the last.

The Strategic Coach Program
For Ambitious, Collaborative Entrepreneurs
You commit to growing upward through three transformative levels, giving yourself 25 years to exponentially improve every aspect of your work and life.

"The Game Changer" is a crucial capability and a natural result of everything we coach in The Strategic Coach Program, a quarterly workshop experience for successful entrepreneurs who are committed and devoted to business and industry transformation for the long-term, for 25 years and beyond.

The Program has a destination for all participants—creating more and more of what we call "Free Zone Frontiers." This means taking advantage of your own unique capabilities, the unique capabilities around you, your unique opportunities, and your unique circumstances, and putting the emphasis on creating a life that is free of competition.

Most entrepreneurs grow up in a system where they think competition is the name of the game. The general way of looking at the world is that the natural state of affairs is competition, and collaboration is an anomaly.

Free Zone Frontier
The Free Zone Frontier is a whole new level of entrepreneurship that many people don't even know is possible. But once you start putting the framework in place, new possibilities open up for you. You create zones that are purely about collaboration. You start recognizing that collaboration is the

natural state, and competition is the anomaly. It makes you look at things totally differently.

Strategic Coach has continually created concepts and thinking tools that allow entrepreneurs to more and more see their future in terms of Free Zones that have no competition.

Three levels of entrepreneurial growth.

Strategic Coach participants continually transform how they think, make decisions, communicate, and take action based on their use of dozens of unique entrepreneurial mindsets we've developed. The Program has been refined through decades of entrepreneurial testing and is the most concentrated, massive discovery process in the world created solely for transformative entrepreneurs who want to create new Free Zones.

Over the years, we've observed that our clients' development happens in levels of mastery. And so, we've organized the Program into three levels of participation, each of which involves two different types of transformation:

The Signature Level. The first level is devoted to your *personal* transformation, which has to do with how you're spending your time as an entrepreneur as well as how you're taking advantage of your personal freedom outside of business that your entrepreneurial success affords you. Focusing on improving yourself on a personal level before you move on to making significant changes in other aspects of your life and business is key because you have to simplify before you can multiply.

The second aspect of the Signature Level is how you look at your *teamwork*. This means seeing that your future consists of teamwork with others whose unique capabilities complement your own, leading to bigger and better goals that constantly get achieved at a measurably higher rate.

The 10x Ambition Level. Once you feel confident about your own personal transformation and have access to ever-expanding teamwork, you can think much bigger in terms of your *company*. An idea that at one time would have seemed scary and even impossible — growing your business 10x — is no longer a wild dream but a result of the systematic expansion of the teamwork model you've established. And because you're stable in the center, you won't get thrown off balance by exponential growth. Your life stays balanced and integrated even as things grow around you.

And that's when you're in a position to transform your relationship with your *market*. This is when your company has a huge impact on the marketplace that competitors can't even understand because they're not going through this transformative structure or thinking in terms of 25 years as you are. Thinking in terms of 25 years gives you an expansive sense of freedom and the ability to have big picture goals.

The Free Zone Frontier Level. Once you've mastered the first four areas of transformation, you're at the point where your company is self-managing and self-multiplying, which means that your time can now be totally freed up. At this stage, competitors become collaborators and it becomes all about your *industry*. You can consider everything you've created as a single capability you can now match up with another company's to create collaborations that go way beyond 10x.

And, finally, it becomes *global*. You immediately see that there are possibilities of going global—it's just a matter of combining your capabilities with those of others to create something exponentially bigger than you could ever have achieved on your own.

Global collaborative community.

Entrepreneurism can be a lonely activity. You have goals that the people you grew up with don't understand. Your family might not comprehend you at all and don't know why you keep wanting to expand, why you want to take new risks, why you want to jump to the next level. And so it becomes proportionately more important as you gain your own individual mastery that you're in a community of thousands of individuals who are on exactly the same journey.

In The Strategic Coach Program, you benefit from not only your own continual individual mastery but from the constant expansion of support from and collaboration with a growing global community of extraordinarily liberated entrepreneurs who will increasingly share with you their deep wisdom and creative breakthroughs as innovators in hundreds of different industries and markets.

If you've reached a jumping off point in your entrepreneurial career where you're beyond ready to multiply all of your capabilities and opportunities into a 10x more creative and productive formula that keeps getting simpler and more satisfying, we're ready for you.

For more information and to register for The Strategic Coach Program, call 416.531.7399 or 1.800.387.3206, or visit us online at *strategiccoach.com*.

THREE LEVELS OF
FREE ZONE FRONTIER

- 100x Collaboration
- Perfect Fit VISION
- 25-Year Hero Target
- 100% Simplifier/Multiplier
- $15-Trillion Free Zone

10X AMBITION

- Self-Multiplying Company
- Simplifier/Multiplier
- Total Cash Confidence
- Always Be The Buyer
- The D.O.S. Conversation

SIGNATURE

- Self-Managing Company
- The Lifetime Extender
- Free, Focus, and Buffer Days
- Unique Ability Teamwork
- The Largest Cheque

FREE ZONE

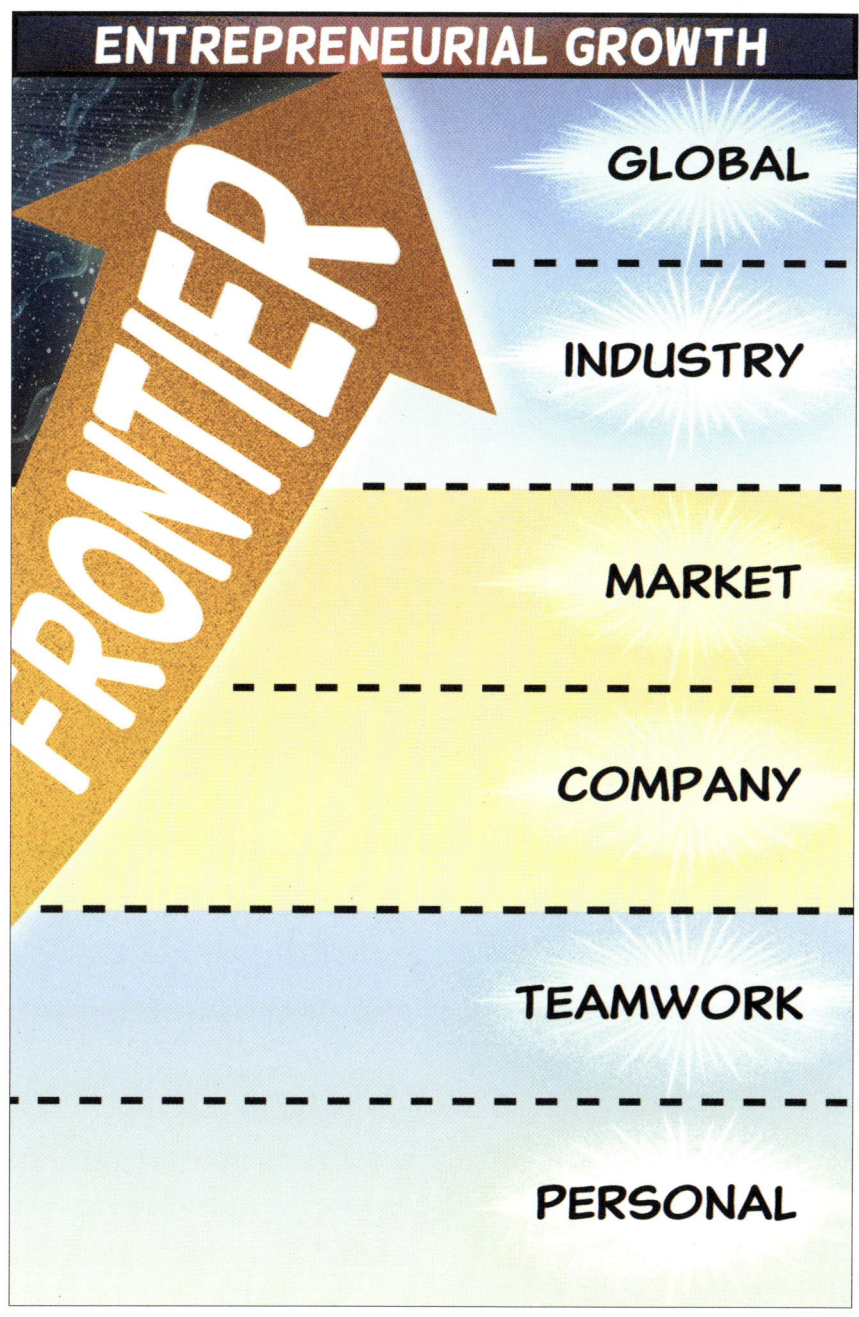

ENTREPRENEURIAL GROWTH

FRONTIER

GLOBAL

INDUSTRY

MARKET

COMPANY

TEAMWORK

PERSONAL

About The Author
Dan Sullivan

Dan Sullivan is the founder and president of The Strategic Coach Inc. and creator of the Strategic Coach® Program, which helps accomplished entrepreneurs reach new heights of success and happiness. He has over 40 years of experience as a strategic planner and coach to entrepreneurial individuals and groups. He is author of over 30 publications, including *The 80% Approach*™, *The Dan Sullivan Question*, *Ambition Scorecard*, *Wanting What You Want*, *The 4 C's Formula*, and *The 25-Year Framework*, and is co-author with Catherine Nomura of *The Laws of Lifetime Growth*.